T0057095

# Mack Wilberg
# Carols

*8 carols for mixed voices*
*by Mack Wilberg*

MUSIC DEPARTMENT

OXFORD
UNIVERSITY PRESS

OXFORD
UNIVERSITY PRESS

198 Madison Avenue, New York, NY, 10016, USA
Great Clarendon Street, Oxford OX2 6DP, England

Oxford University Press is a department of the University of Oxford.
It furthers the University's aim of excellence in research, scholarship,
and education by publishing worldwide

Oxford New York
Auckland Bangkok Buenos Aires Cape Town Chennai
Dar es Salaam Delhi Hong Kong Istanbul Karachi Kolkata
Kuala Lumpur Madrid Melbourne Mexico City Mumbai Nairobi
São Paulo Shanghai Taipei Tokyo Toronto

Oxford is a registered trademark of Oxford University Press

Copyright © 2007, Oxford University Press, Inc, assigned to Oxford University Press 2010

Database right Oxford University Press (maker)

First published 2007

All rights reserved. No part of this publication may be reproduced,
stored in a retrieval system, or transmitted, in any form or by any means,
without the prior permission in writing of Oxford University Press,
or as expressly permitted by law. Enquiries concerning reproduction
outside the scope of the above should be sent to the Music
Department, Oxford University Press, at the address above

Permission to perform the works in this anthology in public
(except in the course of divine worship) should normally be obtained
from the American Society of Composers, Authors and Publishers (ASCAP),
One Lincoln Plaza, New York, NY 10023, or its affiliated Societies in each
country throughout the world, unless the owner or the occupier of the
premises being used holds a license from the Society

Permission to make a sound recording must be obtained in advance from
The Harry Fox Agency, 711 Third Avenue, New York, NY, 10017,
or its affiliated Societies in each country throughout the world.

9 10 8

ISBN 978-0-19-387016-1

Music origination by
Barnes Music Engraving Ltd, East Sussex, England

Printed by Halstan and Co. Ltd., England, on acid-free paper

# Contents


Index of Alternative Accompaniments and Orchestrations iv

Available Recordings v

Carol to the King 1

Gloria tibi Domine 14

How far is it to Bethlehem? 28

Infant Holy, Infant lowly 35

Lullee, lullai, lullo, lullabye 40

Still, still, still 47

The Virgin Mary had a baby boy 52

What shall we give? 64

# Index of Alternative Accompaniments and Orchestrations

Scores and orchestral parts are available on hire from the publishers or for sale as indicated below.

*Carol to the King*

- Piano duet and percussion (snare drum, triangle, bass drum, suspended cymbal, tambourine, chimes, glockenspiel; or snare drum only); (vocal scores with parts available on sale: 978–0–19–386975–2)
- Orchestra: picc.2.2.2.2–4.3.3.1–timp.–3 perc.–strings–harp–optional organ (hire)

*Gloria tibi Domine*

- Piano duet (978–0–19–386914–1)
- Brass (2 trumpets, horn, 2 trombones, tuba), timpani, percussion, and organ (hire).

*How far is it to Bethlehem?*

- 2 flutes and harp or piano (vocal scores with parts available on sale: 978–0–19–386425–2)
- 2 flutes, 2 oboes (opt.), strings, and harp or piano (hire)

*Infant Holy, Infant lowly*

- Strings (hire)

*Still, Still, Still*

- Piano or organ duet (978–0–19–386927–1)
- Strings (hire)

*The Virgin Mary had a baby boy*

- Piano duet, shaker, congas, and double bass (vocal scores with parts available on sale 978–0–19–386929–5)
- Orchestra: picc.1.1.1.1–0.3(opt.).3 (opt.).0–steel drums or piano, percussion, and strings (hire)

*What shall we give?*

- Orchestra: 3.2.2.2–4.0.0.0–harp, and strings (hire)

Please contact the publishers for a full catalogue of Oxford music by Mack Wilberg.

# Available Recordings

*Carol to the King*

• DVD 'Christmas with the Mormon Tabernacle Choir and Orchestra at Temple Square: Volume 2' (available at www.mormontabernaclechoir.org)

*Gloria tibi Domine*
*Lullee, Lullai, Lullo, Lullabye (SATB and organ)*

• CD 'Cantate Hodie: Sing Forth this Day' (Clarion, CLR 903 CD)

*How far is it to Bethlehem?*
*What shall we give?*

• CD 'A Mormon Tabernacle Choir Christmas' (available at www.mormontabernaclechoir.org)

*Infant Holy, Infant Lowly*
*Still, Still, Still*
*The Virgin Mary had a baby boy*

• CD 'Sing, Choirs of Angels' available at www.mormontabernaclechoir.org)
• CD 'Simple Gifts' by Bryn Terfel (Deutsche Grammophon B0004772-02)

## Acknowledgements

The publishers gratefully acknowledge the help of Ralph Woodward in preparing some of the single piano accompaniments.

*for the Mormon Tabernacle Choir, Craig Jessop, Music Director*

# Carol to the King

## (A Christmas Processional)

Jim Christian

French Carol
arr. MACK WILBERG

* Bass part may also be sung by second tenors here.

Copyright © 2006 and 2007, Oxford University Press, Inc.

This collection copyright © 2007, Oxford University Press, Inc.

21
Bear-ing news of joy and glad-ness "Christ, the King of heav'n is born."
25
sim.
An-gels, too, re - sound the an-them To the child-ren of the earth,
sim.
29
Call-ing all to hear the ti-dings Of the bless-ed Sav - ior's birth,

33
Hear them sing, "Ta - ra - ra, ta - ra - rè - re, Li - tam -
36
- pon, la - dé - ri - tam - pon," the fife and an - gel voi - ces ring.
40
sim.
"Ta-ra - ra, ta-ra-ra, ta-ra - rè - re, Li - tam - pon, la-dé - ri - tam -
sim.

44
unis.
- pon," they all re - joice with songs they sing to bring the world a new-born
48
King!
52
mf
S.
A.
Feel the mu - sic stir your sen - ses Like a might - y trum - pet call,
TENORS
T.
mp
mf

56
sim.
Wak - en - ing the world from slum - ber Call - ing out to one and all,
sim.
60
From the vil - lage, from the coun - try Let us join the ho - ly throng,
64
As we hast - en to the man - ger That we, too, may join the song.

68
mf
S.
A.
As we sing, "Ta-ra-ra, ta-ra - rè - re, Li - tam - pon, la-dé-ri - tam -
T.
B.
mp
72
sim.
- pon," the fife and an - gel voi - ces ring. "Ta-ra -
sim.
76
- ra, ta-ra-ra, ta-ra - rè - re, Li - tam - pon, la-dé-ri - tam - pon," we all re -

80
- joice with songs they sing to bring the world a new - born
83
King!
87
ff
92

97
102
106
mf
110
cresc.
114
118

122
f
S.
A.
En - ter now the ho - ly sta - ble To be - hold the bless - ed sight,
T.
B.
f
ff
f
126
sim.
This is Christ, the Lord, the Sav - ior, Pure and filled with ho - ly light,
sim.
130
Tune your heart to hear His mu - sic, Feel the glo - ry of His love,

134
Let us wor-ship and a-dore Him, Won-drous Child of God a-bove.
138
ff
Raise your voice, "Ta-ra-ra, ta-ra - rè - re, Li-tam - pon, la-dé-ri-tam -
ff
142
- pon," the fife and an - gel voi - ces ring. "Ta-ra -

146
-ra, ta-ra-ra, ta-ra - rè - re, Li - tam - pon, la-dé-ri - tam - pon," they all re -
150
- joice with songs they sing to bring the world a new-born King!
155
ff
"Ta - ra - ra, Li - tam - pon, la - dé - ri - tam -
ff
ff

160
- pon, Ta - ra - ra, Li - tam -
165
mf molto cresc.
- pon, We all re - joice with songs we sing to tell us all to rise and sing to bring the
mf molto cresc.
mf
cresc.
170
ff
world a new - born King,
ff
ff

175
— a new - born King,
180
a new - born King!
185
sfz

*Commissioned by the Barlow Endowment for Music Composition at Brigham Young University for the Bach Choir of Pittsburgh and Pittsburgh Symphony Brass, Brady Allred, Conductor*

# Gloria tibi Domine

15th-cent. English carol

MACK WILBERG

Copyright © 2005 and 2007, Oxford University Press, Inc.

17
glo - ri - a ti - bi Do - mi - ne Qui na - tus es de vir - gi - ne.
21
(upper voices equally divided a3)
Glo - ri - a ti - bi Do - mi - ne, glo - ri - a ti - bi Do - mi - ne,
25
S.
A.
glo - ri - a ti - bi Do - mi - ne Qui na - tus es de
T.
B.
T./B.
unis. mf
A

28
vir - gi - ne.
lit - tle child there is y-bore, a lit - tle child there is y-bore, Y -
(born)
32
T.
B.
- sprong - ge out of Jes - se's more To save all us that were for-lore.
(sprung from an offshoot of Jesse)
(lost)
36
mf
S.
A.
Glo - ri - a ti - bi Do - mi - ne, glo - ri - a ti - bi Do - mi - ne,

40
glo - ri - a ti - bi Do - mi - ne Qui na - tus es de vir - gi - ne.
44
Glo - ri - a ti - bi Do - mi - ne, glo - ri - a ti - bi Do - mi - ne,
48
glo - ri - a ti - bi Do - mi - ne Qui na - tus es de vir - gi - ne.
f
52

55
B.
BASS
mf
Je -
59
- sus that is so full of might, Je - sus that is so full of might, Y -
mf
63
- bore he was a - bout mid-night The an - gels sung with all here might,
(their)
67
mf
T.
B.
Je - sus is that chil - de's name, Je - sus is that chil - de's name,

71
Maid and mo - ther is his dame And so our sor - row turned to game.
(parent)
(rejoicing)
75
mp
S.
A.
Glo-ri - a ti - bi Do - mi-ne, glo-ri - a ti - bi Do - mi-ne,
p T. only
T.
Glo - (o) - (o) - ri - a, glo - (o) - (o) - ri - a,
79
glo-ri - a ti - bi Do - mi-ne Qui na - tus es de vir - gi-ne.
glo - (o) - (o) - ri - a, glo - (o) - (o) - ri - a,

83
Glo-ri-a ti-bi Do-mi-ne, glo-ri-a ti-bi Do-mi-ne,
glo-(o)-(o)-ri-a, glo-(o)-(o)-ri-a,
mp
87
glo-ri-a ti-bi Do-mi-ne Qui na-tus es de vir-gi-ne.
glo-(o)-(o)-ri-a, glo-(o)-(o)-ri-a,
91
mf
S.
A.
Glo-ri-a ti-bi Do-mi-ne, glo-ri-a ti-bi Do-mi-ne,
T.
glo-(o)-(o)-ri-a, glo-(o)-(o)-ri-a,
p
mf
p
mf
B.
Glo-ri-a, glo-ri-a,

95
glo-ri-a ti-bi Do-mi-ne Qui na-tus es de vir-gi-ne.
glo-(o)-(o)-ri-a, glo-(o)-(o)-ri-a,
p mf
glo-ri-a, na-tus es de vir-gi-ne.
99
Glo-ri-a ti-bi Do-mi-ne, glo-ri-a ti-bi Do-mi-ne,
glo-(o)-(o)-ri-a, glo-(o)-(o)-ri-a,
p mf p mf
Glo-ri-a, glo-ri-a,
8va
mf bell-like

103
glo-ri-a ti - bi Do - mi-ne Qui na - tus, qui na - tus, qui
glo - (o) - (o) - ri - a, Qui na - tus, qui na - tus, qui
p
mf
glo - ri - a, Qui na - tus, qui na - tus, qui
(8va)
107
na - tus es de vir - gi - ne.
na - tus es de vir - gi - ne.
na - tus es de vir - gi - ne.
(8va)
f

111
S.
A.
S./A.
unis. f
Three
unis.
T.
B.
T./B.
f
116
kings there came with here_ pre-sence, three kings there came with here_ pre-sence, Of
(their)
120
myrre and gold and frank - en-sence As clerk - es sing_ in here se-quence.

124
Set we down up - on___ our knee, Now set we down up - on___ our knee, And
128
pray that child that is___ so free, And with good heart___ now sing we:
132
Glo-ri - a ti - bi Do - mi-ne, glo-ri - a ti - bi Do - mi-ne,

136
glo-ri-a ti-bi Do-mi-ne Qui na-tus es de vir-gi-ne.
140
Glo-ri-a ti-bi Do-mi-ne, glo-ri-a ti-bi Do-mi-ne,
144
glo-ri-a ti-bi Do-mi-ne Qui na-tus es, qui

148
na - tus es, qui na - tus es, qui na - tus es, qui
152
na - tus es_ de vir - gi - ne.
157
fp unis.
cresc.
Glo - - -
fp unis.
cresc.
p sub.
molto cresc.

161
ff
- ri - a, glo - ri - a,
ff
ff
165
unis.
glo - ri - a ti - bi Do - mi-ne Qui na - tus es, qui na - tus es, qui
unis.
169
unis.
ff
na - tus es de vir - gi - ne.
unis.
ff
gliss.
mf
ff

*for the Mormon Tabernacle Choir, Craig Jessop, Music Director*

# How far is it to Bethlehem?

Frances Chesterton

English Carol
arr. MACK WILBERG

The words of Frances Chesterton are set to music and reproduced by permission of A. P. Watt Limited on behalf of The Royal Literary Fund.

Copyright © 2001 and 2007, Oxford University Press, Inc.

16
star? Can we see the lit - tle child, is he with -
20
- in? If___ we lift the wood - en latch, may we go
24
in?
28

* stagger breathing

42
ti - ny hand will He a - wake? Will He know we've come so far
47
just for his sake?
52
cresc.

* stagger breathing

66
brought. For all wea - ry child - ren Ma - ry must weep,
71
(end Baritones)
Here, on the bed of straw, sleep, child - ren, sleep.

Alto (Soprano ad lib.)
75
mp
A.
God in his mo - ther's arms; Babes in the byre
mp
79
Sleep, as they sleep who find Their heart's de - sire.
rit.
Meno mosso
83
mp
poco rit.
a tempo
rit.
89
p

*for the Mormon Tabernacle Choir, Craig Jessop, Music Director*

# Infant Holy, Infant lowly

W żłobie leży
trans. Edith M. G. Reed (1885–1933)*

Polish Carol
arr. MACK WILBERG

* First published in *Music and Youth* (Vol. 1, no. 12, December 1921)

Copyright © 2004 and 2007, Oxford University Press, Inc.

14
poco cresc.
know - ing Christ the Babe is Lord of all. Swift-ly wing - ing an-gels
poco cresc.
18
sing - ing, No-wells ring - ing, tid-ings bring - ing: Christ the Babe is Lord of
22
p
poco rit. a tempo
all. Christ the Babe is Lord of all.
p
mp

26
31
S.
A.
pp
Flocks were sleep - ing, shep-herds keep - ing Vi - gil
T.
B.
pp
35
till the morn-ing new Saw the glo - ry, heard the sto - ry, Tid-ings
pp

39
p
poco cresc.
of a gos-pel true. Thus re - joic - ing, free from sor - row, Prais-es
p
poco cresc.
pp
p
poco cresc.

43
mf
pp
voic - ing, greet the mor - row: Christ the Babe was born for you.
pp
mp
decresc.

poco rit.
47
p
S. only
Christ the Babe was born for
T. only
p
was born, born for
poco rit.
p
a tempo (but slightly slower)
rit.
51
S.
you.
T.
you. Christ was born for you.
a tempo (but slightly slower)
rit.

*Commissioned by the Barlow Endowment for Music Composition at Brigham Young University for the Bach Choir of Pittsburgh and Pittsburgh Brass; Brady Allred, Conductor*

# Lullee, lullai, lullo, lullabye

## (O who will come and listen this night?)

David Warner

MACK WILBERG

Copyright © 2006 and 2007, Oxford University Press, Inc.

* Rhyme with "lullabye"

a tempo
SOPRANO
(40)
mp
O who will come and won - der this hour At one bright
mp Celestes and flutes
Ped.
Man. to Ped., soft 8'
46
star held up by His pow'r To lead us all from our
51
poco rit.
wan - der-ing ways? Come close be - side the Shep - herd to stay.
poco rit.

a tempo
(56)
mp
S.
A.
p
Lul - lee, lul - lai, The shep - herds do
T.
B.
p
60
poco rit.
sigh. Lul - lee, lul - lai, lul - lo, lul - la - bye.
a tempo
(64)
SOPRANO (SOLO or SEMI-CHORUS)
mp
O who will come to His moth - er so mild Who knows the
mp
Man to Ped. 8'
(double pedalling optional)
70
path of her in - no-cent Child that leads to where none

75
poco rit.
oth - er de - scends? Come fol - low Him that her heart may mend.
poco rit.
(80)
a tempo
p
S.
A.
pp
Lul - lee, lul - lai, The mo - ther will
T.
B.
pp
84
poco rit.
cry. Lul - lee, lul - lai, lul - lo, lul - la - bye.
(88)
a tempo
mf
S.
T.
O who will come and watch through the night, And
mf
Ped.
Man. to Ped. 8' & soft 8'
(double pedalling optional)

93
wait on Him who suf - fers our plight, That ris - ing, we may
99
poco rit.
end - less-ly feast? Come, see the morn - ing star in the east.
(104)
a tempo
p
S.
A.
pp
Lul - lee, lul - lai, Come all now draw
T.
B.
pp

108
nigh. Lul - lee, lul - lai, lul - lo, lul - la -
112
SOPRANO (SOLO or SEMI-CHORUS)
mp
Lul - lee, lul - lai, Come all now draw nigh. Lul -
S.
A.
mp
p
- bye. Lul - lee, lul - lai, Come all now draw nigh. Lul -
T.
B.
p
p
+16'
117
molto rit.
pp
- lee, lul - lai, lul - lo, lul - la - bye.
pp
- lee, lul - lai, lul - lo, lul - la - bye.
molto rit.
pp
pp

*for the Mormon Tabernacle Choir, Craig Jessop, Music Director*

# Still, still, still

David Warner

Austrian Carol
arr. MACK WILBERG

Copyright © 2006 and 2007, Oxford University Press, Inc.

13
Ma - ry,_ breath-less, draws Him, weep-ing, To her heart made pure for_ keep-ing.
mp
mf
17
Still,__ still,__ still, His_ bright eyes_ soft - ly__ close.
p
21
26
S./A. p unis. sempre
S.
A.
Sing,_ sing,_ sing, He_
p

31
hears and sweet - ly smiles. And kneel - ing, Jo - seph joins in cho - rus
mp
35
With the an - gels bend - ing o'er us. Sing, sing, sing, He
mf
39
hears and sweet-ly smiles.
mp
44

49
p espr.
S.
A.
Sleep, sleep, O sleep. He breathes a sigh
T.
B.
Sleep, sleep, sleep, He breathes a ten - der sigh, For
mp
mp

53
For soon He'll wake from slum-ber, Bring-ing life and end-less won-der,
soon He'll wake the world from slum-ber, Bring-ing life and end-less won-der,
f

57
Sleep, sleep, O sleep. He breathes a ten - der sigh.
Sleep, sleep, sleep. He breathes a ten - der sigh.
mf
mp
62
67
poco rit.
a tempo
rit.
pp
ppp
pppp
S.
A.
Sleep, Ho - ly Je - sus, sleep, sleep, sleep.
T.
B.
pp
ppp
pppp
poco rit.
a tempo
rit.
p
p
pp

# The Virgin Mary had a baby boy

Trad. West Indian Carol
arr. MACK WILBERG

Copyright © 2006 and 2007, Oxford University Press, Inc.

13
Vir - gin Ma - ry had a ba - by boy, the Vir - gin Ma - ry had a
16
unis.
ba - by boy, the Vir - gin Ma - ry had a ba - by boy, And they
19
said that his name was Je - sus. He come from the
22
glo - ry, He come from the glo - ri - ous King - dom,

25
He come from the glo - ry, He come from the
28
glo - ri - ous King - dom.
31
S.
A.
S./A.
mf unis.
The Wise Men saw where the
34
ba - by was born, the Wise Men saw where the ba - by was born, the

37
unis.
Wise Men saw where the ba-by was born, And they said that his name was
40
Je - sus. He come from the glo - ry,
43
unis.
He come from the glo-ri-ous King-dom, He come from the
46
glo - ry, He come from the glo-ri-ous King-dom.

49
S.
A.
Oh, yes, be - lie - ver, Oh,
T.
B.
52
unis.
yes, be - lie - ver, He come from the glo - ry,
unis.
55
He come_ from the glo - ri - ous King - dom,

57
unis.
He come from the glo - ry, He come from the
unis.
60
glo - ri - ous King - dom, glo - ri - ous King - dom, glo - ri - ous, glo - ri - ous,
63
unis.
come from the glo - ri - ous, glo - ri - ous King - dom.

65
f
Yes, be-lie - ver,
f
f
68
Yes, be-lie - ver,
Yes, be-lieve, and they
71
said that his name was Je - sus. The an - gels sang when the

74
ba-by was born, the an - gels sang when the ba-by was born, the
77
an - gels sang when the ba-by was born, and they said that his name was
80
unis.
Je - sus. He come from the glo - ry,
unis.

83
unis.
He come from the glo - ri - ous King-dom, He come from the
unis.
86
glo - ry, He come from the glo - ri - ous King-dom.
89
Oh, yes, be - lie - ver, Oh,

92
unis.
yes, be - lie - ver, He come from the glo - ry,
unis.
95
He come from the glo - ri - ous King-dom, He come from the
unis.
unis.
98
glo - ry, He come from the glo - ri - ous King-dom,

101
glo - ri - ous King - dom, glo - ri - ous, glo - ri - ous,
103
ff
Yes,
He come from the
ff
sfz p sub. cresc.
sfz
106
glo - ri - ous King - dom, glo - ri - ous King - dom,
ff

108
glo - ri - ous, glo - ri - ous King - - -
sfz p sub. cresc.
111
unis.
- dom.
He come from the,
unis.
sfz
114
He come from the, come from the glo - ri-ous, glo - ri-ous King - dom!
sfz

*for the Mormon Tabernacle Choir, Craig Jessop, Music Director*

# What shall we give?

David Warner

Catalonian Carol
arr. MACK WILBERG

**With a slight lilt, but not too fast**

Copyright © 2001 and 2007, Oxford University Press, Inc.

10
tam, pa-tan, tan - tam; tam, pa-tan, tam, pa-tan, tam, pa-tan-tam;
13
tam, pa-tan, tam, pa-tan, tam, pa-tan, tan - tam; tam, pa-tan, tam, pa-tan,
16
tam, pa-tan - tam;
mf
19
8va

22
(8va)
loco
25
TENOR
mp
T.
What shall we give to the Boy in the tem - ple? What shall we of - fer the
mp
28
Man by the sea? Palms at His feet and ho - san - nas up - ris - ing,
31
are these for Him who will car - ry the tree? Tam, pa-tan, tam, pa-tan,

34
tam, pa-tan, tan - tam; tan, pa-tan, tam, pa-tan, tam, pa-tan-tam;
37
S.
mf
Tam, pa-tan, tam, pa-tan, tam, pa-tan, tan - tam; tam, pa-tan, tam, pa-tan,
T.
mf
Tam, pa-tan, tam, pa-tan, tam, pa-tan, tan - tam; tam, pa-tan, tam, pa-tan,
mf
40
tam, pa-tan-tam.
tam, pa-tan-tam.
f

43
47
S.
A.
p
What shall we give to the
T.
B.
p
mp
50
Lamb who was of - fered, ris - ing the third day and shed - ding His Love?

53
Tears for His mer - cy we'll weep at the man - ger; bath - ing the In - fant come
56
down from a - bove. Tam, pa-tan, tam, pa-tan, tam, pa-tan, tan - tam;
p
59
tam, pa-tan, tam, pa-tan, tam, pa-tan-tam; tam, pa-tan, tam, pa-tan,
mf
mf
mf

* stagger breathing

68
ff
(ah)
ff
ff
ff
(8va)
ff
71
p
p
p
p
(8va)
loco
mp

74
poco rit.
77
a tempo (but slightly slower)
rit.
pp
S.
A.
Tam, pa-tan, tam, pa-tan, tam, pa-tan-tam, pa-tan - tam, pa-tan-tam, pa-tan -
T.
B.
pp
a tempo (but slightly slower)
rit.
p
80
a tempo
rit.
- tam.
a tempo
rit.